Professor Wooford McPaw's
History of Cars

Elliot Kruszynski

Hiya Prof! Ok, let's take a look at what's inside this book.

You see I first became interested in cars when I was a young pup and I –

Yes, alright Prof – shall we cut the waffling and get on with it?

BC (Before Cars)

It is hard to imagine what life was like before there were cars. Once you had to work where you lived. You could only eat food that was grown nearby. If you moved away from your hometown, you would very possibly never see your friends and relatives again. Cars give us the freedom to travel where we like when we like. We can cross cities in an hour and an entire continent in a few days!

So who invented the first car?

Well actually the car was invented in stages. As far back as the 15th century, people imagined building a vehicle that would harness energy to move at great speeds.

Boing!

In 1478, Leonardo DaVinci imagined a cart that would drive itself using springs.

In 1492, Roberto Valturio designed a cart with windmills attached to its wheels.

In the Netherlands in 1600, it is said that a vehicle with two sails attached, carrying 28 people, reached speeds of 30 km/h.

In 1748, a carriage propelled by a giant clockwork engine was constructed by the French inventor, Jacques de Vaucanson.

The Age of Steam

The first proper automobile was built in 1759 by a French inventor called Nicolas-Joseph Cugnot.

It was a tricycle with a steam engine, which worked like this: Water was heated in a boiler, creating steam. The steam pushed pistons, which turned a crankshaft connected to the wheels, moving the vehicle.

This is the life

Cugnot's tricycle is said to have run for 20 minutes at 3.6 km per hour.

Erm... I can actually walk faster than that!

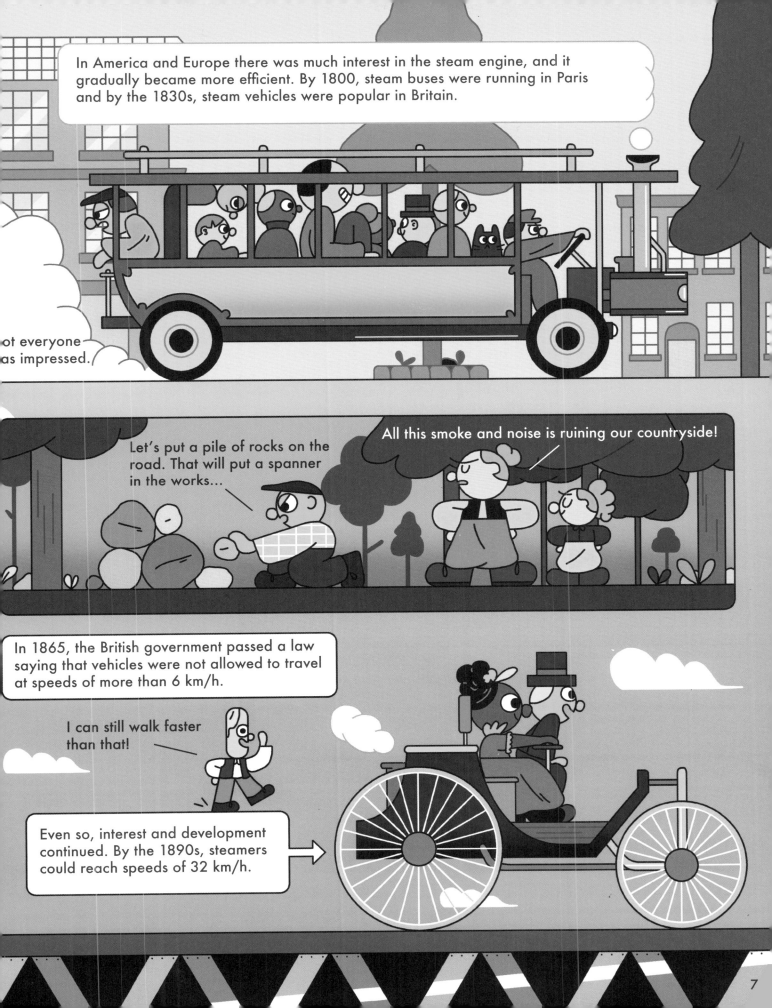

In America and Europe there was much interest in the steam engine, and it gradually became more efficient. By 1800, steam buses were running in Paris and by the 1830s, steam vehicles were popular in Britain.

ot everyone as impressed.

Let's put a pile of rocks on the road. That will put a spanner in the works...

All this smoke and noise is ruining our countryside!

In 1865, the British government passed a law saying that vehicles were not allowed to travel at speeds of more than 6 km/h.

I can still walk faster than that!

Even so, interest and development continued. By the 1890s, steamers could reach speeds of 32 km/h.

Bend it Like Benz

In 1876, Nikolaus Otto invented the four-stroke combustion engine.

This engine ran on a type of fuel called gasoline (or petrol). It was safer and easier to use than the steam engine.

In 1888, Karl's wife, Bertha, became the first person to drive the car over a long distance.

Without telling Karl, she and her two sons drove

During her trip, Bertha encountered many problems, for which she had to improvise solutions.

...and located fuel at a city pharmacy in Wiseloch (the world's first gas station).

invented brake lining...

She insulated wires using garters...

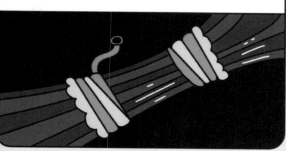

Her inventions were incorporated into future designs.

A German inventor called Karl Benz was greatly inspired by Otto's engine.

He developed it with obsessive passion, spending all his (and other people's) money building a three-wheeled car with a combustion engine. The car was unveiled in 1885, but people were still sceptical that it would ever take off.

106 km across southern Germany in two days.

Proving to the public what a useful contraption the automobile could be.

Against all odds, Karl Benz's 'motorwagen' grew in popularity, and by the 1890s, other companies across France, Italy, Britain and the USA began building automobiles with combustion engines.

You might think of the electric car as a recent invention, but in fact electric engines were being developed alongside combustion engines as early as the 1890s, and for a while they were a lot more popular. Hey Mrs Tab, can you show us some facts about early electric cars?

Electric Vs. Gasoline

Of course Prof! Here are some facts I've just found.

They are less noisy, less smelly and easier to operate. And they start without having to crank the engine by hand. I do so hate a handcrank.

Here we have one of the first electric cars made in England by Thomas Parker in 1895.

In London and New York City there were soon fleets of electric taxis.

They proved to be very popular in America. We can see here how much of the US population drove electric cars by the turn of the century.

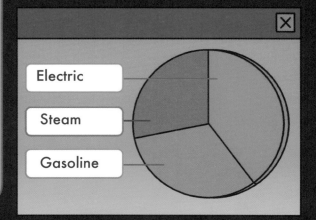

Electric

Steam

Gasoline

Alas, I must confess all is not perfect with one's electric vehicle.

However, there were some major drawbacks. They could only travel 80 km before their batteries ran flat, and they were not efficient at speeds over 30 km/h.

In 1912, the electrical starter for a combustion engine was invented, making them easier to use.

New discoveries of oil brought gasoline prices down.

And finally, a man called Henry Ford began making gasoline cars that cost about half that of an electric car.

At that price one just can't say no. Ta raaa!

By the 1930s, electric cars were a thing of the recent past... and the distant future. Hope that helped, Prof!

In the early years of the 20th century, cars were popular, but they were also very expensive.

In 1908, Henry Ford designed a car called the Model T, which he manufactured using pre-made parts on a moving assembly line.

You see every worker has a specific task and then the car moves onto the next worker.

This was a very efficient way of working: Fewer workers were needed and they could operate much more quickly.

The time it took to make a car went from 12.5 hours to just 1.5!

Cadillac Runabout, 1902 – A stylish and reliable horseless carriage with a single cylinder engine.

They don't make them like this any more!

Mitsubishi Model A, 1917 – The first car manufactured in Japan. It was so expensive that it went out of production after four years, and no more passenger cars were made in Japan until 1960.

Wow, what a selection! Let's have a look at some of these old models and see how they've changed over the years.

Please don't lean on me.

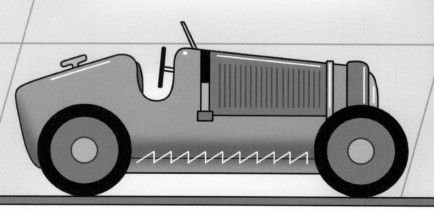

Bugatti Type 35, 1924 – The most successful racing car of its time, with a distinctive arched radiator. It won 1,000 races and set 47 world records.

So cool!

Buick Runabout, 1901 – Engine innovations made this car faster and more efficient, but only six were sold!

I bet mine goes faster

Model T Ford, 1908 – Also known as the 'Tin Lizzie' this was the first mass-produced, affordable automobile, and it turned the car from a luxury into a necessity.

Lancia Lambda, 1922 – One of the most advanced pre-war cars. It featured a light, low body, suspension and four-wheel brakes.

wow

Chrysler Airflow, 1934 – The first car to use streamlined design to reduce air resistance.

How Does a Car Work?

Hmm... good question. Well, erm i think...

Don't worry, Prof, I've got this covered. Let's take a look inside me!

1 The outer shell of the car is called the body. It is usually made of steel, but some are made of strong plastics, carbon-fibre or fibreglass.

2 The driver presses on pedals to make the car move and stop, and turns the steering wheel to guide the car where they want it to go.

3 Most cars are powered by internal combustion engine which converts energy from burning fuel into power the propels a car. It works like this:

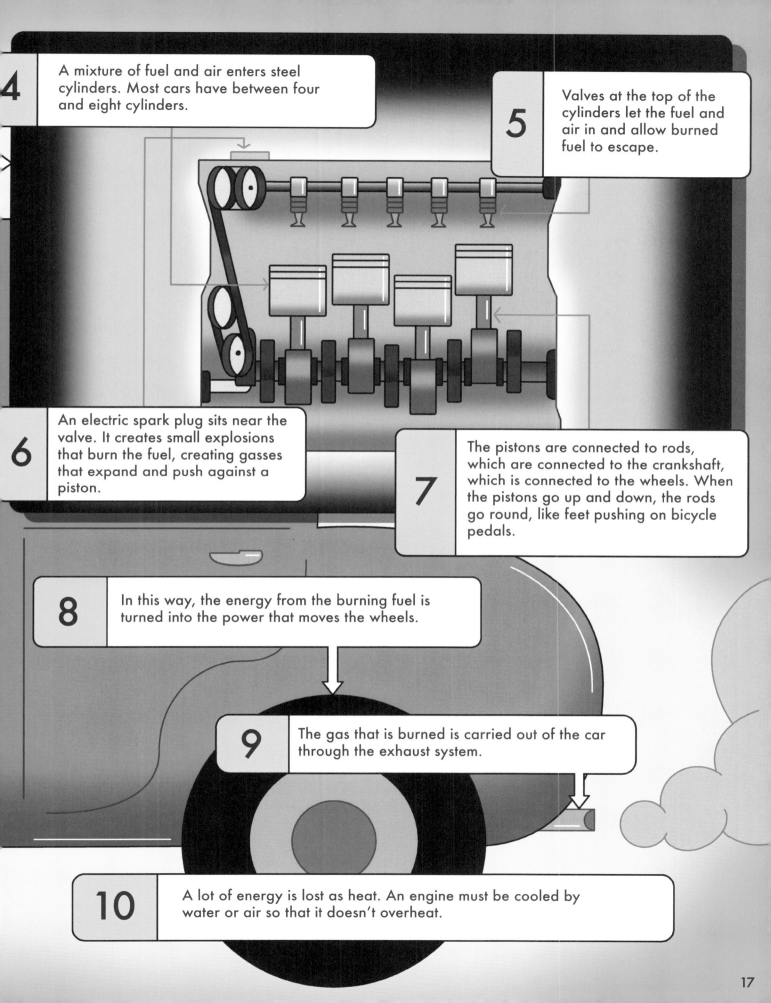

4 A mixture of fuel and air enters steel cylinders. Most cars have between four and eight cylinders.

5 Valves at the top of the cylinders let the fuel and air in and allow burned fuel to escape.

6 An electric spark plug sits near the valve. It creates small explosions that burn the fuel, creating gasses that expand and push against a piston.

7 The pistons are connected to rods, which are connected to the crankshaft, which is connected to the wheels. When the pistons go up and down, the rods go round, like feet pushing on bicycle pedals.

8 In this way, the energy from the burning fuel is turned into the power that moves the wheels.

9 The gas that is burned is carried out of the car through the exhaust system.

10 A lot of energy is lost as heat. An engine must be cooled by water or air so that it doesn't overheat.

Practical Post-War Cars

Taking their cue from Ford, European nations rushed to set up their own affordable car industries. By the 1930s, there were many car manufacturers all over Europe. France had Citroen, Peugot and Renault, Italy had Fiat, Alfa Romeo and Lancia and England had Morris, Rover and Rolls Royce – to name a few.

During the Second World War, most car manufacturing stopped so that the factories could produce military vehicles, but it resumed in the mid-1940s, after the war.

The Story of the Volkswagen Beetle

In 1937, Adolf Hitler commissioned car designer Ferdinand Porsche to build a cheap, reliable car for German workers; a 'people's car'. Porsche created a distinctive, curvy design with the engine in the back.

It looks a bit like a funny little beetle!

I find that offensive.

A factory was built to manufacture these 'Beetles', but as soon as war broke out, it had to make military vehicles instead.

But we did make some Beetles for military officers and Hitler was given the first convertible.

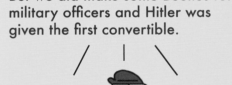

After the war, the factory, which had been heavily bombed, was put under the control of a British officer called Major Ivan Hirst.

I'm going to start manufacturing Beetles again. Would any of you like to buy the factory?

You must be joking! It's a hideous car and the factory is in ruins! You're wasting your time.

Against all odds, Hirst managed to breathe new life into the factory, reviving the clever design by Porsche.

By the end of 1946, around 10,000 Beetles were manufactured. A decade later, one million had been sold.

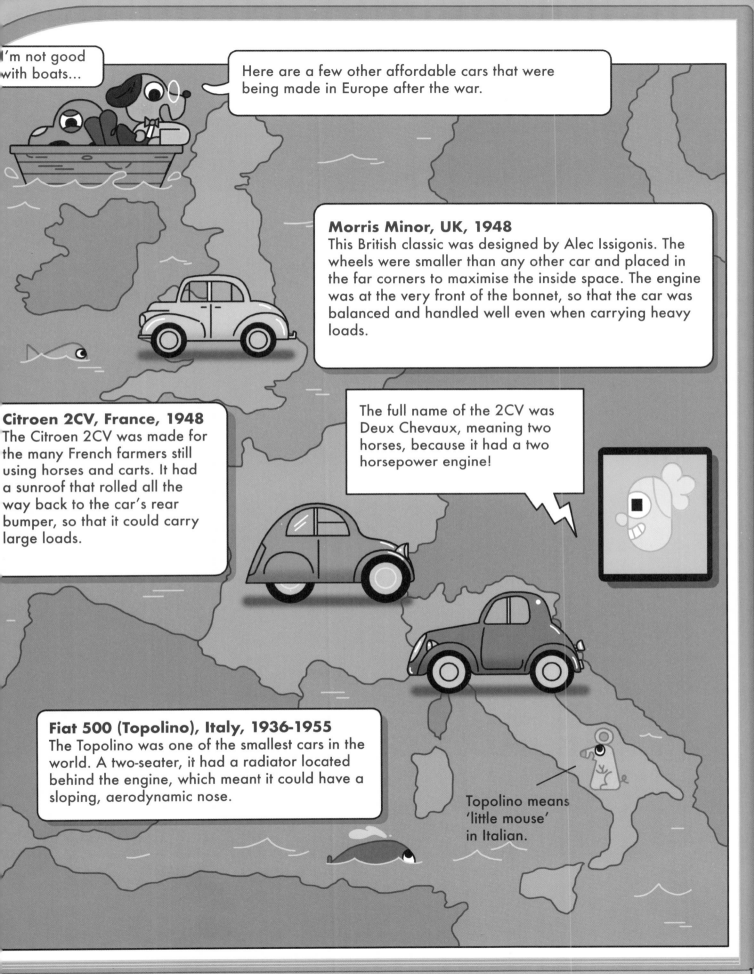

I'm not good with boats...

Here are a few other affordable cars that were being made in Europe after the war.

Morris Minor, UK, 1948
This British classic was designed by Alec Issigonis. The wheels were smaller than any other car and placed in the far corners to maximise the inside space. The engine was at the very front of the bonnet, so that the car was balanced and handled well even when carrying heavy loads.

Citroen 2CV, France, 1948
The Citroen 2CV was made for the many French farmers still using horses and carts. It had a sunroof that rolled all the way back to the car's rear bumper, so that it could carry large loads.

The full name of the 2CV was Deux Chevaux, meaning two horses, because it had a two horsepower engine!

Fiat 500 (Topolino), Italy, 1936-1955
The Topolino was one of the smallest cars in the world. A two-seater, it had a radiator located behind the engine, which meant it could have a sloping, aerodynamic nose.

Topolino means 'little mouse' in Italian.

But not everyone wanted an affordable car. As the economy of the 1950s boomed, so did the market for luxury cars. In Europe, car-makers like Rolls-Royce and Mercedes developed expensive cars with powerful, smooth-running engines. The interiors were decorated with velvet, leather and polished wood.

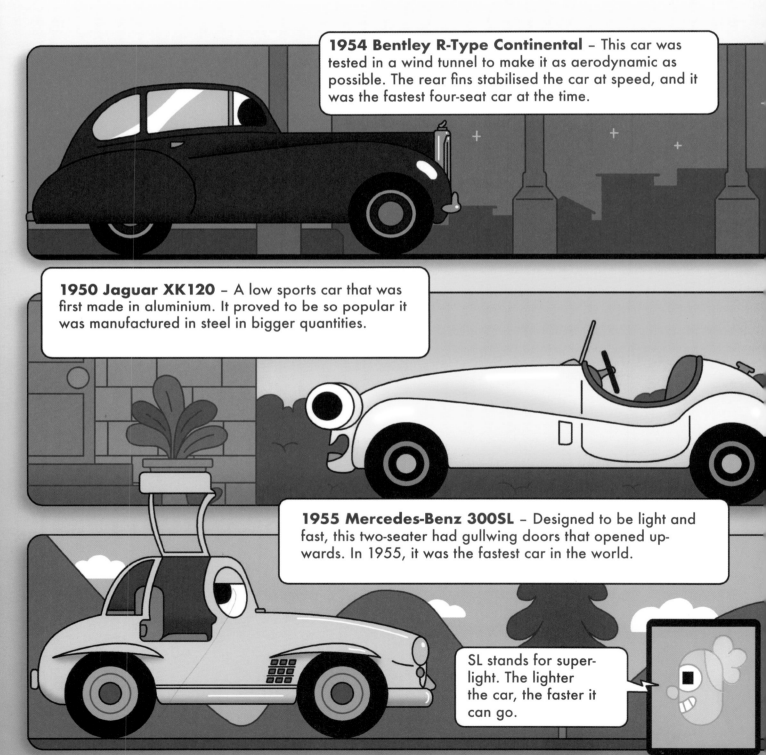

1954 Bentley R-Type Continental – This car was tested in a wind tunnel to make it as aerodynamic as possible. The rear fins stabilised the car at speed, and it was the fastest four-seat car at the time.

1950 Jaguar XK120 – A low sports car that was first made in aluminium. It proved to be so popular it was manufactured in steel in bigger quantities.

1955 Mercedes-Benz 300SL – Designed to be light and fast, this two-seater had gullwing doors that opened upwards. In 1955, it was the fastest car in the world.

SL stands for superlight. The lighter the car, the faster it can go.

In America, the luxury cars were a bit different. Gasoline had become very cheap and car-makers started designing huge cars, known as gas guzzlers. These cars were inspired by the design of airplanes and often had chrome details and decorative fins.

I'm looking for something big. Real big.

1950 Pontiac Cheftain Catalina – This car was so luxurious It included a powerful radio, tissue dispensers, under-seat heaters and an electric shaver.

1957 Chevy Bel Air – Known as 'the Hot One' this was a striking car with lots of chrome, a low roof and wheel covers.

1959 Cadillac Eldorado Biarritz – This vast car weighed 3000 kg and measured six metres long. With its raised, narrow fins it looked like a rocket ship.

This one is as heavy as a hippopotamus. Is that big enough for you?

Early motor racing

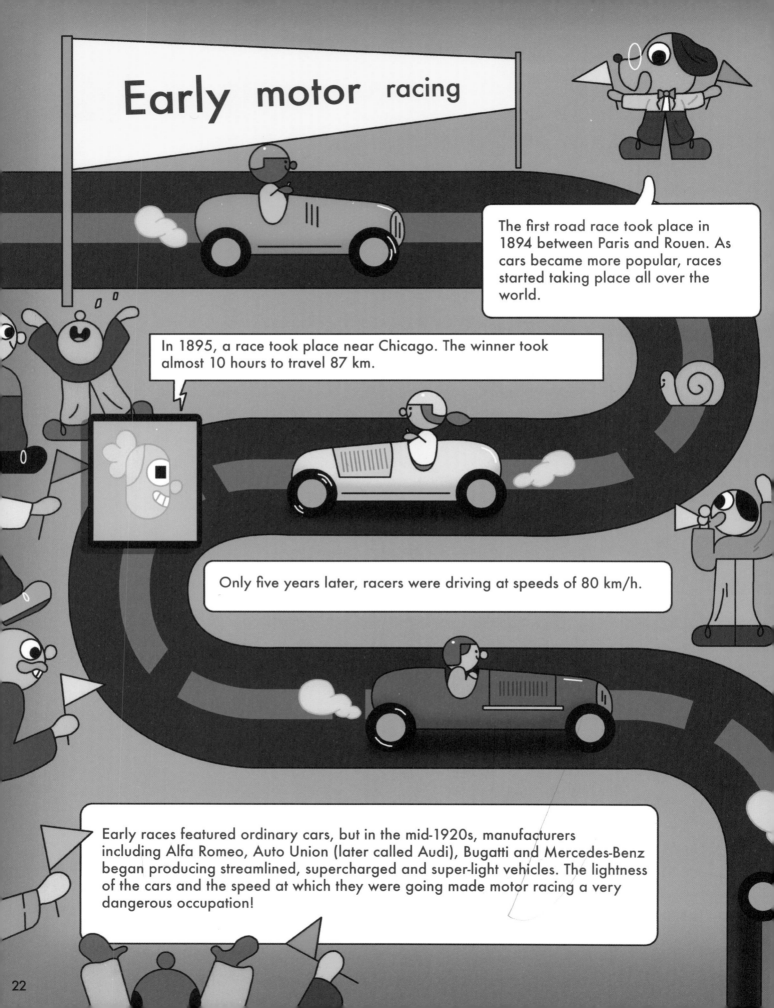

The first road race took place in 1894 between Paris and Rouen. As cars became more popular, races started taking place all over the world.

In 1895, a race took place near Chicago. The winner took almost 10 hours to travel 87 km.

Only five years later, racers were driving at speeds of 80 km/h.

Early races featured ordinary cars, but in the mid-1920s, manufacturers including Alfa Romeo, Auto Union (later called Audi), Bugatti and Mercedes-Benz began producing streamlined, supercharged and super-light vehicles. The lightness of the cars and the speed at which they were going made motor racing a very dangerous occupation!

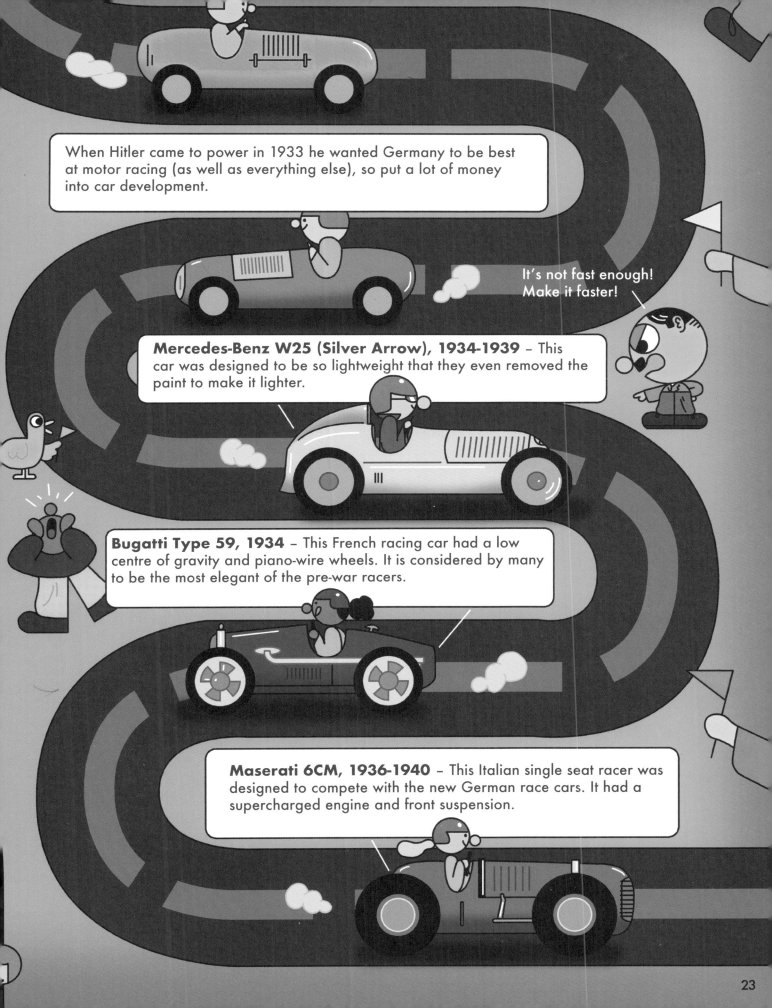

When Hitler came to power in 1933 he wanted Germany to be best at motor racing (as well as everything else), so put a lot of money into car development.

It's not fast enough! Make it faster!

Mercedes-Benz W25 (Silver Arrow), 1934-1939 – This car was designed to be so lightweight that they even removed the paint to make it lighter.

Bugatti Type 59, 1934 – This French racing car had a low centre of gravity and piano-wire wheels. It is considered by many to be the most elegant of the pre-war racers.

Maserati 6CM, 1936-1940 – This Italian single seat racer was designed to compete with the new German race cars. It had a supercharged engine and front suspension.

Motor Racing Today

As the cars became more sophisticated, so did the races. Many races that were established after the Second World War are still going on today.

Grand Prix

Grand Prix races involve single seat cars with open wheels. They take place on racecourses or on regular roads that are closed to the public.

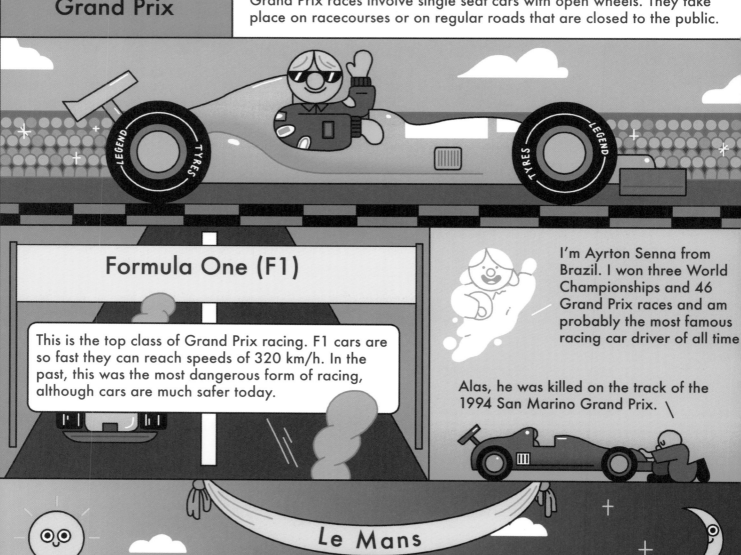

Formula One (F1)

This is the top class of Grand Prix racing. F1 cars are so fast they can reach speeds of 320 km/h. In the past, this was the most dangerous form of racing, although cars are much safer today.

I'm Ayrton Senna from Brazil. I won three World Championships and 46 Grand Prix races and am probably the most famous racing car driver of all time

Alas, he was killed on the track of the 1994 San Marino Grand Prix.

Le Mans

Le Mans is a Grand Prix race established in 1923. The race lasts for 24 hours and the car that drives the furthest in that time, wins. The deadliest race ever was the 1955 Le Mans. A Jaguar braked suddenly, causing a car behind to be flung into a crowd of spectators, where it exploded into flame, killing 84 people.

Stock Car Racing

Stock car racing is popular in the USA. These races take place on paved tracks and use normal cars that have been souped up with powerful engines that can reach 300 km/h.

Rallies

Rallies take place on public roads with two people inside the car – a driver and a navigator. The route of the rally is unknown until the race begins. Sometimes it covers thousands of miles.

Drag Races

In drag races, drivers compete to see who can accelerate the fastest from a standing start. Top dragsters can reach 400 km/h in a matter of six or seven seconds.

The Modern Car and the Rise of Japan

By the 1970s, cars had lost some of their glamour. Fuel prices were rising, and people started to worry about safety and pollution.

Pollution? What nonsense. People want big, sturdy cars with powerful engines.

Ford

GMC

Chrysler

1969=35c per gallon

1974=60c per gallon

1981=$1.31 per gallon

Some manufacturers began making smaller, lighter, more fuel-efficient cars called compacts. Two companies in Japan began competing fiercely with each other for this market. Nissan produced a small, cheap family car called the Bluebird, whilst Toyota made a similar car called the Corona.

The two companies fought it out, spending a lot of money on researching and developing new features that would put their car at the front of the race. This led to the Japanese cars becoming extremely efficient and reliable – and very good value.

Before long, Japanese cars were taking the American and European markets by storm. By the 1980s, Japan was producing 13 million cars per year – the most in the world.

We keep costs down by only making the parts that we need when we need them. It's called the just-in-time method.

I have a small engine and light parts, so I'm fuel efficient but still fast.

Manufacturers around the world raced to catch up. Most of the cars on the roads today were inspired by the Japanese models of design and manufacturing.

Sedan – A closed automobile seating four or more people.

Minivan – A taller, box-shaped car with sliding doors and additional backseats to fit larger families.

Stop barking or I'll turn this car around!

Coupe – A two door car with two sporty seats at the front and a very small backseat (or none at all).

Modern Cars

Convertible – A car with a retractable roof, which is usually stored in the trunk. Sometimes the roof is made of fabric and sometimes it's a hardtop.

SUV – Standing for 'Sports Utility Vehicle', this car is big and rugged, designed for driving off-road. It has a high driving position with a good view of the road and four-wheel drive for traction on muddy tracks.

Sports car – A powerful car built for speed on normal roads. It is low to the ground, so that it stays stable when turning corners at high speeds. It has sleek, aerodynamic lines and a big engine that can accelerate quickly. It often only has two seats.

Alternatives to Gasoline

By 1986, there were half a billion cars in the world, and concerns about pollution became more real. In the 1990s, governments said that cars had to become cleaner and more efficient.

Coff Coff, I can't breathe!

You must become cleaner and more efficient.

At first diesel seemed like the answer. Diesel is a very efficient type of fuel, so you can drive further using less of it. But by 2012, it became clear that this efficiency came at a price.

Diesel fuel releases particles called nitrous oxides that have terrible effects on health.

Car companies said that they had found ways of creating 'clean diesel' but it turned out this was not true, and that they had been cheating on the emission tests.

Problem solved!

EMISSIONS
100
0

BIOFUELS

Biofuels are possibly a better alternative...

Biofuels burn oils from crops or algae, rather than petroleum, and could be cleaner and more sustainable than regular fuel.

There are some problems with biofuels too. If we use crops that could otherwise be used for food, this could lead to food shortages.

Also, we need to take into account the environmental impact of growing the biofuel – did we get more energy out of the oil than we put into growing it?

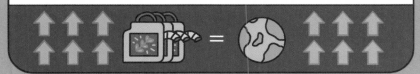

HYDROFUELS

Hydrogen fuel cells generate power by splitting hydrogen molecules and then combining them with oxygen.

They produce no emissions except water, and could offer a way of creating a completely clean car.

Unfortunately, hydrogen is explosive, so they could be dangerous. Also, the methods used to produce hydrogen and its expensive transportation costs make it less ecologically sound than one would hope.

Hydrogen fuel cell cars are therefore still in early stages of development.

Electric Cars

In 1997, Toyota produced a 'hybrid car' called the Prius, which had an electric motor with a combustion engine alongside it.

In the 1990s, a new battery was developed called the lithium ion battery. This was lightweight and lasted a long time. Suddenly electric cars became a real possibility.

Two for the price of one!

Depending on driving conditions, hybrid cars use either only the motor, or both the engine and the motor, consuming much less fuel and producing fewer emissions.

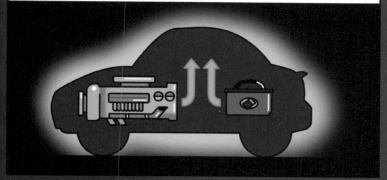

In 2008, an entrepreneur called Elon Musk developed an all-electric car called the Tesla Roadster, which could drive 300 km on a single charge.

Pack in more batteries! I want the whole floor to be one big rechargeable battery!

At first, completely electric cars were very expensive and not very environmentally friendly to produce. But as more companies developed them, the prices started coming down and they became greener to make. There are now over six million all-electric cars in the world. They are efficient, quick to charge and can travel up to 500 km before they run flat.

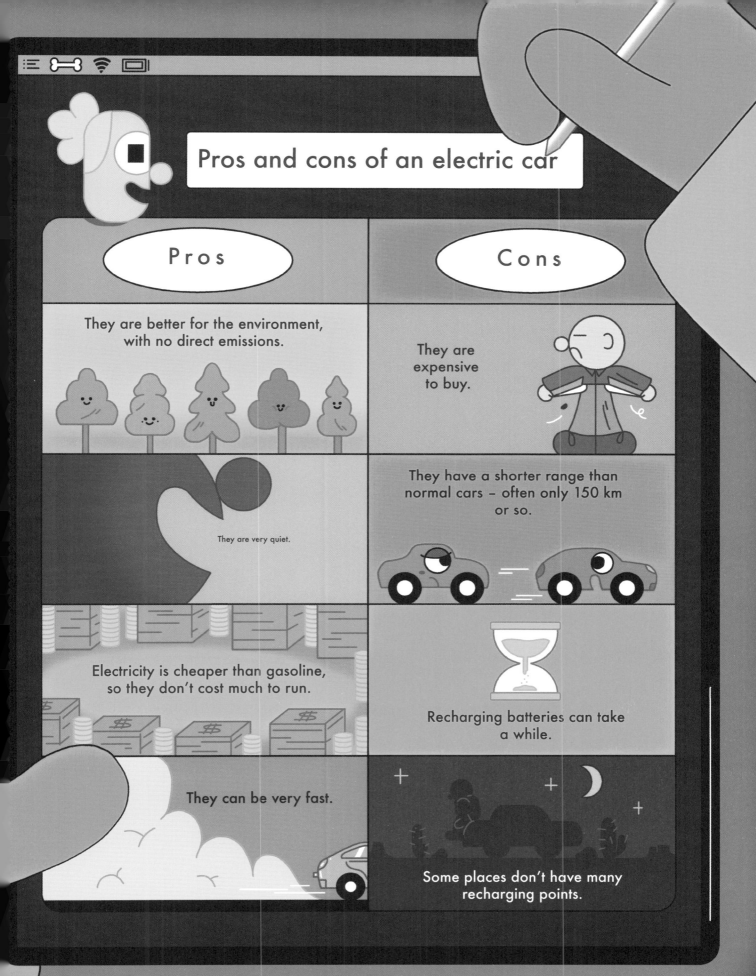

Pros and cons of an electric car

Pros

They are better for the environment, with no direct emissions.

They are very quiet.

Electricity is cheaper than gasoline, so they don't cost much to run.

They can be very fast.

Cons

They are expensive to buy.

They have a shorter range than normal cars – often only 150 km or so.

Recharging batteries can take a while.

Some places don't have many recharging points.

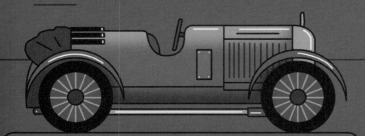

Bentley Speed 6
1926–1930

One of the most successful early racing cars.
Its long bonnet hid a gigantic engine.

Jaguar E-Type
1961–1975

This sleek sports car was designed to be
super light and weighed a mere 1315 kg.

These are my favourite sports cars of all time.
Don't touch them – they're my very precious
toys, ahem, I mean collectables!

Porsche 911
1963–Today

A two-door, championship-winning sports car
that, apart from some modifications, has
remained unchanged through the ages.

Aston Martin DB5
1963–1965

A luxury grand tourer (GT) car, designed for high speed and long distances. It was made famous by the James Bond movie, *Goldfinger*.

Lamborghini Miura
1966–1973

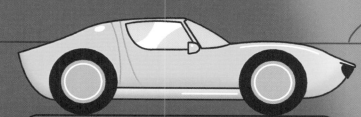

The first supercar to feature a rear mid-engined two-seat layout.

Ferrari F40
1987–1992

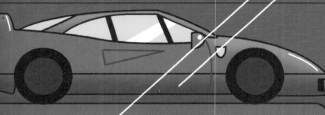

Engineered by the infamous Nicola Materazzi, this was Ferrari's fastest, most powerful and most expensive car.

McLaren P1
2013–2015

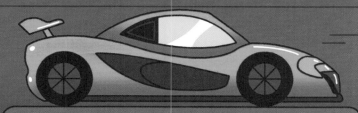

This million dollar, 903 horsepower hybrid car was inspired by the shape of a sailfish. Only 375 were ever made.

Do not touch!

Cars of the Future

Since the car was invented 130 years ago, there have been many developments and improvements. Cars today are safer, quicker and more environmentally friendly than they used to be. But there are also lots and lots and LOTS of them.

There are over one billion cars in the world today, and that number is growing all the time.

With so many cars, it is important that traffic runs seamlessly. Most cars are already connected to the internet. In the coming decade, vehicles will be able to communicate with each other and with the roads and infrastructure around them, making journeys safer and quicker. Self-driving cars will pick their way around hazards and through traffic with no human input. Smart traffic lights and junctions will keep traffic flowing smoothly.

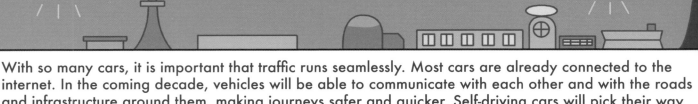

My route says I'll be turning left soon.

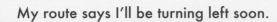

I'm going straight, so I'll give you space to move into the left lane.

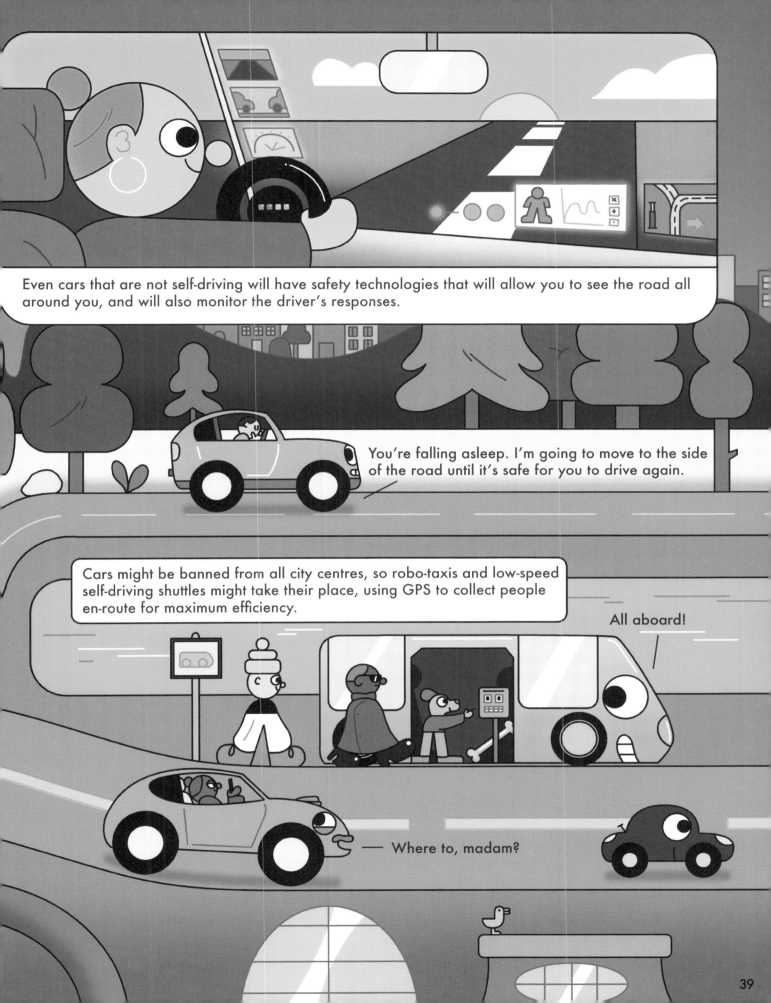

Even cars that are not self-driving will have safety technologies that will allow you to see the road all around you, and will also monitor the driver's responses.

You're falling asleep. I'm going to move to the side of the road until it's safe for you to drive again.

Cars might be banned from all city centres, so robo-taxis and low-speed self-driving shuttles might take their place, using GPS to collect people en-route for maximum efficiency.

All aboard!

Where to, madam?

The Weirdest Cars of All Time!

A car has to be functional, powerful and efficient. And it has to look snazzy, so that people will pay money to drive it! A few car designers through the ages might have got a little bit carried away with their visions...

Ouef Electric, 1942
The 'electric egg' was a three-wheeled bubble of aluminium and plastic. It ran on batteries at a time when electric cars were very unfashionable.

Citroen Karin, 1980
A concept car that featured a pyramid design with butterfly doors and a three-seat layout with the driver sitting in the middle and a passenger on either side.

Nice style!

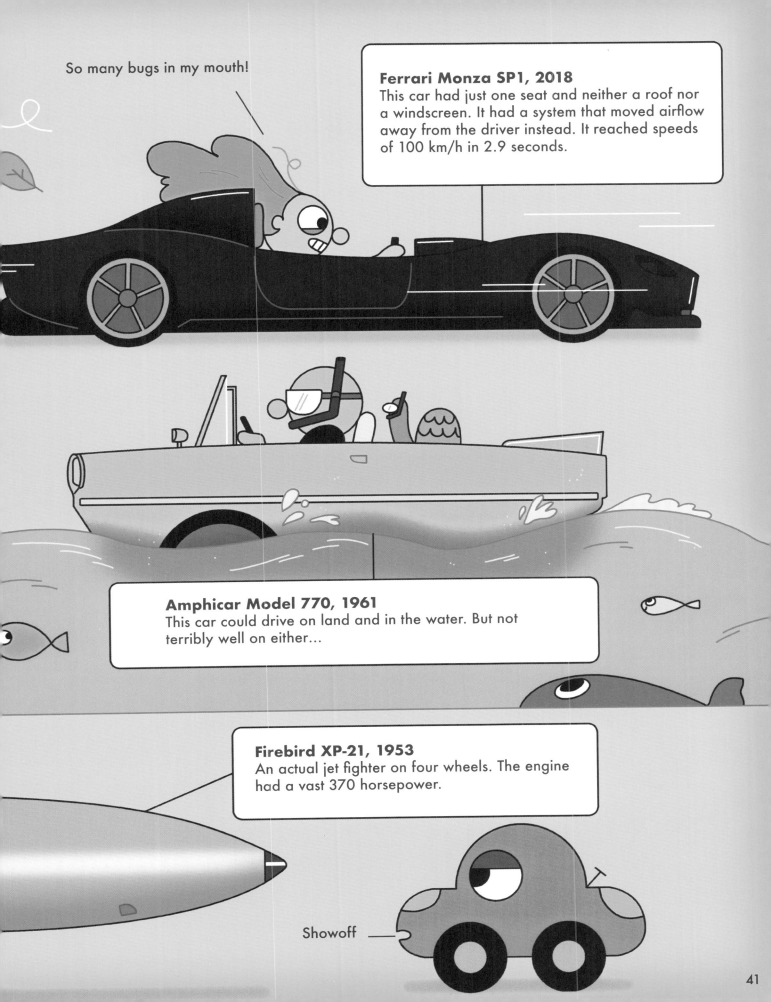

So many bugs in my mouth!

Ferrari Monza SP1, 2018
This car had just one seat and neither a roof nor a windscreen. It had a system that moved airflow away from the driver instead. It reached speeds of 100 km/h in 2.9 seconds.

Amphicar Model 770, 1961
This car could drive on land and in the water. But not terribly well on either...

Firebird XP-21, 1953
An actual jet fighter on four wheels. The engine had a vast 370 horsepower.

Showoff

Well, thanks so much for reading! Hopefully you are now an expert on all things cars. I'm off to do some research on the history of astronomy. I'm thinking about writing another book one day about this most fascinating of subjects. Did you know that the moon is shaped like a lemon? And also...

Sorry about him, he really does go on sometimes. I've hidden five of his precious golden bones throughout the book. Why don't you see if you can go back through and find them all?

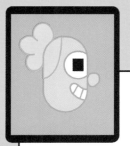

If you need any help finding anything in this book, please use this nifty index

Professor Wooford McPaw's History of Cars

Text © Elliot Kruszynski and Ziggy Hanaor
Illustrations © Elliot Kruszynski

British Library Cataloguing-in-Publication Data.

A CIP record for this book is available from the British Library.
ISBN: 978-1-908714-95-4
First published in 2021

Cicada Books Ltd
48 Burghley Road
London, NW5 1UE
www.cicadabooks.co.uk

Printed in China

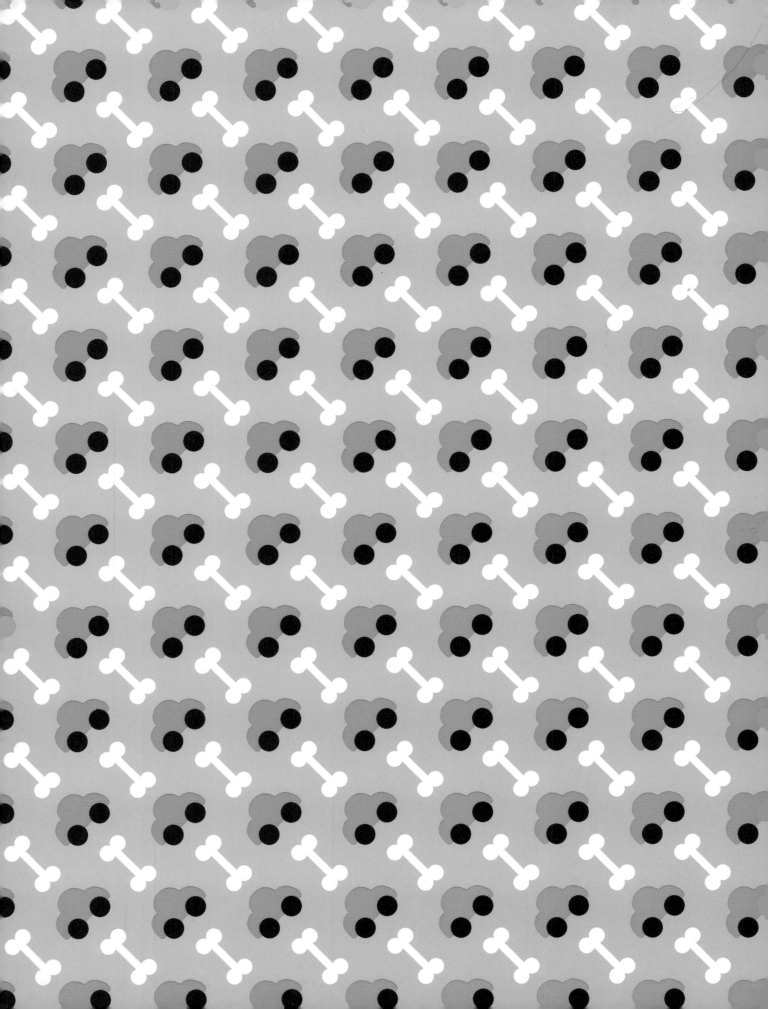